DOWN AND OUT

T.K. Waits

Sideshow Media Group
8033 Sunset Blvd. #164
Hollywood, CA. 90046
sideshowmediagroup.com

© 2016 T.K. Waits
ISBN: 9780997129700

All rights reserved. No portion of this book may be reproduced, stored in a retrieval system, or transmitted in any form or by any means electronic, mechanical, photocopy, recording, scanning, or other - except for brief quotations in critical reviews or articles, without the prior written permission of the publisher.

Published in Los Angeles, California, by Sideshow Media Group

Bulk copies of this book can be ordered by contacting:

Sideshow Media Group
8033 Sunset Blvd. #164
Hollywood, CA. 90046
info@sideshowmediagroup.com

Sideshow Small Books are inspired by *The Pocket Poetry Series* that **City Lights Bookstore** in San Francisco released to reinforce the work of Beat Poets.

They are designed to:

A) Fit into someone's back pocket so that they can be used in emergency situations

B) Be left in locations that are in need of poetry

MONDAY.

imagine the rain

falling hotter than

the fires of hell

hitting the tin roof

a cadence even

heavens marching band

couldn't play

the clouds will

devour the sunlight

starving for darkness

easing into tomorrow

the last days are near

moving swiftly like

the foxes do

don't run child

stay for a minute

watch the forests burn

listen to the tune

the rabbits sing

when the flames

come rolling in

while the ocean

sprints away descending

eager to return

throwing our waste

back into our faces

stay for awhile

put the coffee on

light a cigarette

God is coming

S.S. HEARTBREAK.

She showed me the lump in her left breast again today

and I felt how it had grown since the summer

I've grown into a slump

A particular type of sadness

I can't explain

It's something

Fucking and

the good whiskey

won't fix

THE DISTANCE.

The dogs haven't been fed today

And fucking with the door open didn't happen much

Don't fret little baby

Because the bastard will be on your steps soon

In that empty place

Pumping life in you

My shorts on the floor

With an open door

I miss you

FOR A FRIEND.

I was somewhere on Portland Avenue when the call came

through

I've never really had to hear it

I was always been there to see

Like when my

My grandmother

My father

His brother

And so on have been

Thrown over the sacred line

And given to the dirt

Walker was smiling when I walked in

He was holding a Playstation 4 controller

And his fascination with the video games made sense to

me in that second

They amuse the boy who's afraid of being unamused for

too long

Or something

I gave the bastard a hug and his beard was damp of tears and tequila

I brought 12 beers and some cheap

Cigars to fill with grass

We walked into an evening together

Holding hands and skipping down nostalgia lane

remembering a man who was a guru of sorts and a champion of a soul

The madness is real

A friend of mine has lost his mind with his life

Stabbing his mother repeatedly then shooting for the stars

Juggling weed smoke and hand grenades.

ALONE AND WELL.

It's maddening to

Remember her

Isn't it

How she'd turn red

When you'd kiss her

The onetwo wiggle

Of her nose

Love chased me

As I chased it

Away with a stick

From the sea to the trees

I'm alone again

Trying to be a writer

Sniffing sensations

And tired

MISS E.

The floodgates opened

And she was poured out

Like open beers from the night before

Wounded and strong he sits

As she spills down the curvature of his cheek Over the

scars left by a better hand and onto a dirt stained wrist

Fante means plenty when he was a God to the bum I call

Jesus

But means more when from a woman who sees the

vultures circling again

Like the ice in my drink and the winds

I will be safe from me

I can promise you that

However will I ever be safe

From you

TONIGHT.

Her blood was burgundy

The California sky in April

And all over

From miles away I've realized im mad

For what makes a man

Secure but knowing his

Insecurities

Like a good whore I should belly the toxics

Swallow my words through a buttonhole

And carry on

Tata and be salty

CHANGES.

As the house fills up with cold air to be warmed by the

breath of the drunks

I am still listening to Lush Life attacking the machine

Still chasing the one I shouldn't be

It's like I never left the woods

I can hardly remember my life

In California and that hurts me

I felt welcomed and warmed surrounded by the sun

And strangers

You can hear a broad yell timber and watch a broken

man push broken to the limits with a fresh pine sent and

shit covered jeans as he leaves the woods for good

A SONG.

I can see that you're

longing belonging to yourself baby

and i hope

you can make it on through

The only thing in life worth

Knowing by now is

Your booze

Your smokes

And you

CENTRAL OREGON NIGHTS.

Waiting on the waiters

Waiting on the cooks

Waiting on the food

It's a madhouse

A game

Another night

On Galveston

LONG GONE.

We slept in different beds

I felt her curves in my sleep

And was excited

The erection

Or my alarm woke me

Around seven this morning

I had to go back into the pines

And wasn't too happy about it

After snapping a picture of her

Brick building

I jumped in the back of a cab

42nd and Harrison

Is where the car to take me

Home rests

HOT BREAKFAST AND PUSSY.

I miss the wrinkles

On her elbows

And find myself

On the shit colored

Couch

The Devil Makes

Three is playing

For the drunks

And whores

The quiet ones

Have found a

Screen to fuck

Slouched and

Wheezing the brave

Listen and cry

The surrogate

Madhouse welcomes

Another Tuesday

Toasting to Monday's

Death

Hot breakfast

And pussy

I'M COMFORTABLE.

The skin fits tight

Tonight

Like the couch cushions

It feels good

It feels right

To hold yourself

So dear

So dear

I've grown tonight

Goodnight

Goodbye

Tata

And

Stay Salty

I LOVE YOU.

She said it in the doorway

Of a room painted a pale blue

I believed it for the first time

Since the first time

THE NOW.

To be lost in the

Wonderland that is

The 21st century

Is a nightmare

Walking in on a rape

Shooting yourself in the foot

Biting the hand that feeds

It's all still so breathtakingly

Black and white

And green

A NOTE.

Pursuing the one you love

Completely ignorant to all else

Is dangerous

Chasing the one you're

Incapable of trusting

Might make you

Mad

BOYS AND GIRLS.

They tried tricking him

Jack and Jill

Spilled their genitals

Over a plastic wrapped lie

Oh baby baby

He fell off his rocker

Somewhere between

Mexico and Canada

And the carpet was

Swept clean

Today

ALMOST DEAD.

We slept well together

Most nights

Last night seemed as

The rest do and did

To tell ya the truth I felt

Pretty damn good

No booze

No grass

Not even a cigarette

Entered my body last night

Living the saints life for

An evening

No harm could be done

Her sleeping pants have

Always had a way of fitting

Around her hips and buttocks

Securely hugging both pairs

Of body parts perfectly

And the cotton covered the

Genetic artwork and the lamp

Went out

It's six or seven in the morning

I'm off of Galveston and Harmon

Don't let me die here kid

I puked

The siracha doused macaroni

Was thrown from my stomach

Sloppily

Violently

Purposely

I heard the symphony strike

For a second while

The lights flooded in

And she yelled for me

A short cab ride from

The riverside house with

The red door

And 20 some odd dollars later

I'm stabbed with a iv and told

About the state of my body

Three bags of magic liquid

To keep me safe from myself

The iv ended up on the bed

Along with my blood and

Softly muttered cursing towards

The staff of the emergency room

In St. Charles Medical Center

On the fifth of September

The year of 2014

MAYBE.

I've given up

On love

The ditch diggers

Shovel has broken

With his back and

Dwindling hope of

Any of us being

The capable

Lovers we are

INEBRIATED FACTS.

My father could

Without a doubt

Babble and slur

About the

"My days"

If he had any

To spare

Most of the

Satin skinned

Women will lie

Filthily through

Corrected teeth

To smile in

The rumbles of

A broken man

TODAY.

The clouds are stagnantly shading the small central

Oregon town

Two minutes from work

And the weariness of the distant

Future rests heavy on my shoulders

For today he may break like waves and fine china

WET DREAM.

She was a ghost woman

With artwork for a body

She sucked me

And put me inside her

I went to grab a breast

And awoke with a handful

Of leather

The couch is warm

And my sweat sticks

My legs and back

To the cushions

My erection bounced

Goodbye to the ghost

I completely woke up

And sang a song

THE MIDDLE.

Between agony and bliss

The bottle is thrown

Crashing silently

Burning quickly

Doing its job

Making the easy days

Easier

And the hard ones

Work

A BAD POEM.

Exchanging hot remorse for five minutes or so she

reminded herself

Why she left in the first place

To predict the unpredictable

Is impossible unless

You're in the wrong place

At the right time

the lighting

Just dim enough

For the lips to find

themselves

A deaf bull in a china shop

Knows not what antiques

Sound like when dropped

Rather the smell of yesterdays

Before broken are identified

With ease

IT'S A BEAUTIFUL THING.

The candy bar

And cigarettes

Have my mind

Feeling ill with

My Stomach

So she feeds me

Roasted turkey breast

On a fine roll with

Bacon and avocado

I smoke a cigarette

She smiled

We argue about

What may have

Happened

What didn't

Happen

It's a beautiful Thing

BEER AND WOMEN.

Beer and Women.

Keep em' from coming

Or

Keep em' from going

THE MUSIC.

Tiss tittit, tiss tittit, badah, dah dum, dooda, bue, bue,

bob, dadah.

The dead music for dying souls

Or what have you

You think Louis ever thought about

The gun

The bottle

St. Peter's smile

Otis is sobbing over

Another woman

With hot breath

Wishing to see

The familiar smile

On a dock

C'mon baby

Let's dance

One last time

Before the city

Steals me for good

TO BE HONEST.

it's a kind distortion

when the ideals

throw bones with

the brash reality

the seconds rust

birds are singing

and somewhere

a woman misses

me

LADY DEATH.

it's the phone ringing again

when I'm not in the mood

for a conversation

the lose whore

on my neck when

i've got a woman

the loaded gun

on a good day

a hungry wallet

and empty stomach

on the bad ones

musing around in

the substances

molding the shit

she's laughing again

through high crossed legs

throwing bottled ships

and blowing kisses

to the wind

fucking anything

breathing and bleeding

the tramp

my little slut

i'm trying to sleep

reminiscing on

the mouth of an angle

or a dime piece named toots

miles from Los Angeles

breathing the pines breath

and puking wine

Tata

SEPTEMBERS HERE.

Put the beauties behind you

Women, mountains, beaches

And trudge into the ugliness

Following the mice

and cockroaches

Helpless

Devoted

To the only

Valuable gift

This world and

Your gods

Have given you

A strong back

A week mind

And a will to exist

Drowning out the sirens

With cheap wine

and cigarettes

SNOW AND BONES.

It was more or less

a drunken stumble

That took me from grace

At a table half covered in

Snow and bones

TRY AND HIDE.

Deaths coming

Quick on the

Left side through

The slop

Towards the fool

Singing the songs

That were made

For the birds

Loading the gun

Hitting the bottle

Bitting the bullet

And leaving the track

Dead or rich

THE GRANDSON.

When I reached the top of that cliff, above the sand caverns, and flourishing greenery dripping with the lazy creek down over the stone face into the stagnate ponds on the floor of a barren riverbed. I knew this sight wouldn't come again for sometime. It's low tide, the sun has nested what looks to be half of itself deep into the ocean. The clouds swirl violently through a pastel sky. Six dolphins beautifully displayed their agility and flipped from the pink ocean, dyed from the sky.

I thought of my father, and how he wanted to see California.

I thought of Hemingway and how he would take knowing Hugh Kirkman's sons son is a fatherless writer.

LONG GONE.

Today I don't

Miss the hours

Of laying within

The blue walls

With the one

I've learned to

Accepting the past

For what it is

Not a damn thing

Yesterdays are

Sitting with the likes

Mandela

Erwin

Vonnegut

And

Pops

Today lives

In bullets

Booze

And bridges

LBC.

The tune of the

Fool

The song of

The clown

The music is roaring

Tonight

The bastard is belting

Bent notes

Curving like her

Breasts from the

Under side up

And shot in the

Heart of the one

That got away

What's it take to

Get way

And

What's the price

Of Chinese tea

The case of my

Only instrument

Is a basket one

And I've been playing

It rough

Nowadays

The birds sing

About my stench

From the open

Window and

The hummingbird

Hasn't been around

Since my finger took

A turn for the worst

The day most mothers

Are acknowledged

As the vessel

That harbored you

Until the lights flashed

The sounds flooded in

And the war

Was started

WITH HOT BREATH.

May the winds kiss

Your lips and send

Love

From the singing fool

Howling the winos blues

MADDIE THE STRANGER.

The cartilage of

Her septum was

Bright and pink

The sun made

A map of veins

In her nose

And I could smell

The ocean and

Wine on my breath

I've never been on

This bridge

Over the port

Or in this car

But I was comfortable

She laughed

And I yelled

And mentioned

Things about Hank

Seeing how we

Happened to be

Slithering through

San Pedro

With then heat

Cooking anything

It touches

Alone in our thoughts

Together in a convertible

With the top up and

The air conditioner on

Walkers Dinner on the

Edge of Sunken City

Or Slab Lands

Which ever you prefer

Is where I happened to pop

Looking for a decent sandwich

DOWN AND OUT

I asked a man

About the history

Of the shack on the cliff

I asked of a Hank

The man laughed

And said

You mean that

Tab that's still

Unpaid in there

And that drunk

Who would babble

About flying here

And there and

Those horrible

Poems

It was

Another brunette

Another Maddie

Another day in

Southern California

SLEEPLESS AND SWEATING.

The shadows will

Make you sweat

Like a whore in church

It's a 101 in Long Beach

I'm on Pine and Fourth

With Cherokee Charlie

The coffee was on him

This morning and has a

Better taste that

The garbage at

The LA Times

California has the most

Violent dog and human

Relationship in the country

Next to New York

Insurance companies

Had thousands of

Canine attack claims

Just this year

And so on

The evening of Mother's Day

I was compelled to

Accept the challenge

Of manliness

Offered by a

Jewish pro surfer

It was a wrestling match

In a ring lined in

Fiberglass surf boards

And wet suits

I achieved manliness

And choked the bastard

A good one

Until his face was

Purple like the veins

In my testicles

Then a let him go

His nap lasted three

Or for seconds

Before I noticed

My ring finger

Had shifted to

The right at the

Second knuckle

At about a

65 degree angel

But I was a man

The pain could wait

So I haven't been

Playing gods work

In the microwave like

Kitchen on

Pine and Broadway

Much as of late

Killing sea roaches

And lobsters for the

Rich and successful

Is what reminds me

Where I stand

Without it

I could maybe

Convince myself

Otherwise

It's dangerous

This time off

Also today's check

Will be starved

The hours of blood and sweat

Are compacted into

7 green pieces of paper

Equaling 130 dollars

That's the booze

and smokes

I'm putting work

Into work

It's a mess

I met Maddie outside

Of LaOpra

On Pine and First

She had just

Gotten off the clock

A petite young woman

21 years old

5 foot 4 inches

90 pounds

In a black dress

Fitting tight around

The chest and waist

Then flowing outward

The type of dress

Old guys hope

The wind takes up

For a small flight

She's an ex circus performer

Who could balance

Head over heals

On six bar stools stacked

Like San Francisco

And could bend her bones

Like notes from a Coltrane tune

And can fit in a suitcase

Well could fit in a suitcase

Until the car crash on

The 5 north that

Ended the career of

Being a freak

A sideshow

And started the

Beginning of a

Normal female human

Adulthood

The sun threw

Stinging punches

All the way from

Long Beach to San Pedro

She's taking me to

See the Sunken City

Hank lived here

I was looking at

Another mans madness

And enjoying it

With a circus sideshow

Is a half dead Doge Sebring

With seats covered in

Cigarette ash and holy

As a preachers suit

I told her about my

Manliness and showed

Her my grape knuckle

She laughed and demanded

That I allow her to

Mother me momentarily

And buy me something to

better the condition of

the finger i'd be better

off without (ring finger, the fuck is that)

She purchased a steel

Blue splint from RiteAid

I asked for

steak and whiskey

FUTURE.

Like Hunter

I know where

And when I'll

Close the portal

To breathing

Whiskey

Cigarettes

And jazz

In a cloud of

Cowboy smoke

Or tied to a stick

Singing old spirituals

And bringing home

The vultures

I'm lost in the streets

Of Harlem with

Langston Hughes

And Louis has

More than the

Saints marching in

Tonight

A WHORE NAMED LUCY.

Thank you,

beautiful bruised woman

A lucky strike brunette

With the eyes if an owl

The Lady of The Night

I watched you

Walk

Walk

Walk away

With that unfair walk

Most women will

Never have

Powerful strides

Sharp and shining

Eight inch stilettos

Kiss the concrete

The body of a

1955 Cadillac

In a black dress

Bending over

With an undercarriage

Of baby blue lace

Exposed to the buyers

The animals

The rent money

Now baby, Lucy

When I'm old

Dying and rich

I'll pay you for

That information

Conversation

With the drunk

Boy in the Skids

Leave a nickel on

Fifth street

And the bottle

Still gives a little

Put the broads

And the bastards

On Vine and Hollywood

And the dream

Still lives

In wine stains

and sirens

JAILS NO PLACE FOR ME.

They should have

Thrown me in

The looney bin

With mattress walls

Stained with

Piss

Shit

Blood

Spit

And

Life

A man hasn't been

Made mad

Until he's caged

Alone

For days on end

With the bed sheet

And the crumbs of

Coffee cake

Bartered with the

Killers

Addicts

Thieves

Gangsters

And

Simply confused

For paper

And reading

Material

The fat kleptomaniac

Stops talking whenever

I tell him I have to shit

Rolling over and facing

DOWN AND OUT

The concrete wall

Of our fully furnished

And all expenses paid

Vacation home

In the heart of

Deschutes County

Central Oregon

You have to flush first

The bright shinning

Steel thrown is set

To a timer

A kind gesture

Is better than

An angry criminal

And a log floating

Unwanted and stinking

For 8 more seconds

Let the fat woman

Swallow the keys

And belt them out

Bent and jagged

To the winds

A man isn't a man

Until he's been

Less than an

Animal

A flesh sack of

Nothingness

In a green suit

Of mildew and disease

Speaking only minimally

Only when spoken to

Madmen racing to

The chair

The men in blue

Pulling the trigger

Clicking the switch

Pushing the button

Living the lie

Open the door

And close the

Door

Over again

Until we're all

Dead

Or

Golden Boys

GOOD MORNING.

Outside is

Grey

The cats are

Sitting in the

Window

Feeling the cold

ocean air

The checks are

In today

And I'm going

To make it

To the track

This weekend

NOW BABY.

The bombing

Of Nagasaki

And Hiroshima

Is Felix's work

You'd know that

If you had read it

In a book somewhere

Covered in

blood and dust

My glass is

Bleeding and

Wild turkeys become

Violent when bottled

Houdini never really

Disappeared

Humans just never

Thought to look

Where he wouldn't be

Like death

Like life

Like me

GROWING OLD ISN'T FOR PUSSIES.

I watched a man

Verbally assure

Himself he wasn't going to

Fall when standing up

From his electric blue

Walking chair

Starch hardened

kaki trousered

Creased and uncreased

Under the spastic legs

Of a human being

Who's well prepared

For the white lights

And his final ride

While persuasively coaching

himself

When bending his knees

And stretching his spine

As straight as possible

"You can stand."

"We can stand."

"You won't fall"

His spine cracked once

And gently returned

to it's bow shape

Suddenly my

Drunken disposition

Brightened up for a

Couple of minutes

While he eased

Away from me

One minuscule

Trembling

Step at a time

Accompanied with

The breath of

Lady Death on the

Back of his neck

HIT ME AGAIN.

They are

After me

Again

Wolves in

Diamonds

Circling the block

Twice

Three times

Four now

Frida has been

Spotted by the

Blood thirsty

Bastards

I'm on the

corner of

Pine and Broadway

Not scared

But nervous

For when the

Attack comes

I won't be ready

But hungry

For the bones

The rights

The lefts

The thirty knuckles

Taking turns on me

Beat my body

To where my mind

Rests and

You might have

Me done

DANCING WITH DEATH.

To spend your last

24 smiling and laughing

All morning into the afternoon

Spending all that's left over

From the cash

You wire to your mother

On drinks and cigarettes

She waits at the Western Union on

Broadway and Main

In Moses Lake, Washington

Wishful thinking and some grass

Have her thinking her boy is

Finally better

At last, he's free

From the blues

You even go

Into work to tell

JP the manager

You may need some

Time off

All the while

Knowing

You'll never cook

Another damn lobster

Today you'll speak

To the women without

Fearing them as a God

The food will taste better

You'll eat slow

Make friends

Put a smile on a face

Drink up

Drunk down

And jump

THE ZITS.

And she would

Smile and laugh

At conversations

Never to be had

Again

I'd lay on my back

And she's start on my

Face

Squeezing

And cursing

Until they were

Freed

LBC.

The poison air

Isn't half as bad

As the creatures

Breathing it

A juggernaut

Civilization

Producing

A vicious

Cannibal youth

Hungry for

What they

Will never

Have

The dream

Is in the wind

Dust like my

Father

And

Dead

A TUNE FOR THE PAGE.

I've left

Humming words

Of songs for

Birds strong

With courage

In the eyes

Of the cat

With a knob

Tail

And some

Missing teeth

His claws take

The life that's

Been beat right

To where the

Cadillacs park

And the ocean

Meets the trees

I KNOW YOU KNOW.

You're missed like

Santa Clause

And

Hearings my fathers

Datsun creep

Into the gravel

Drive way to

That dead old

House

On Rainier and Valley

That's where The fire started

Where I learned

To love the

Women

Where I began teaching

Myself the music

Of the pen

Its gone nowadays

A barren lot

In the

Cascade Valley

Of Moses Lake

Washington State

Gone

Like you are

Absent in all the

Loveliness

I've been trading

The sandman grass

For dreams

In which you're there

Sitting in front of

A cafe

Under an umbrella

At a steel

mesh topped table

With a cup of

Coffee

Equipped with

A foam leaf

Or some

Bullshit

My angle baby

My angle baby

LET HER GO.

Tangled in

The hair of

Your lovers

Last kiss

Winter Winds

Howl at a velvet

Sky

On the train ride

Home

And the fox

He just roams

And the fox

He just roams

this morning from about

1:00am until about 6:00 am

A victim of an old habit

sits welcoming the sunrise

from the roof of the flat on

28th and St. Lewis

saying goodnight

to the day to come

as the drunkenness

creeps over me with

the cool sheets

the floor is nome enough

when home is ashes and ideas

swept under the rug

in front of the front door

a swirling Neapolitan sky

waked up God's children

and the elderly first

it's a sunday

it's six in the morning

i work in eleven hours

i need a rest

or

more blow

i awoke about

11:00am

the cold sheet

of last night is

warm and wet

with sweat

i'm weary as to

what might had

happened the night

prior

i remember Kim

the asian girl

with the good legs

who sat nervously

amongst the partying

i lost Kim

to a hispanic boy

a young football player

with hair steps

a letterman jacket

and a scholarship

down in Florida

for throwing a ball

sometimes winning isn't

everything

when you've got 24 or so beers

and cigarettes lasting into

next week

you're winning enough

DOWN AND OUT

the morning traffic is

arguing with the birds

and i remember

there was an awful

god awful

party last night

the males bragged

more than the

whore nagged

and i'm growing

sick of what i've

made myself endure

recalling of the

mad

mad

scene

28TH AND ST. LOUIS.

I am boarding

The 22 buss

Running with

The winds on

Ocean and Cherry

Dramamine and alcohol

Have got me thinking

I should

Slow down

Hit the brakes

Settle down

Wrap it up

Be cool

Move along

Pull the plug

Or something

I've got almost

Half a thousand dollars

And an empty refrigerator

There are holes in

My mattress filled

With bottled dreams

And liquid courage

The menace was

Freed this morning

A handful of magic

And a throatful

Of modern medicine

Have me gawking

At exotic women

Covered in make up

With beauty matching

That of a

Los Angeles sunrise

breaking through

The skyline

Unnatural and raw

With a case

Of the

Fuck yous

HEADING TO WORK.

In order to clean up

you've gotta

get a little

messy

And heavens

to Betsey,

That I'll

Be at my best

see you at

The track with

a pint and a

Pack of

Cigarettes

I SHOULD'VE BEEN A SONG WRITER.

Bill from London

Is wrinkled with leather skin

and moves

In a shaking manner

Tells the people passing

"Fuck off with your

Californian dream

This state has died with

Kennedy."

Ed from Rhode Island

Is drinking whiskey

From a flask hidden in

A hollowed out bible

He told me four times now

"I like my whiskey

Like my women

Uncorked, aged, and on coke"

Cherokee Charlie

Is reading the paper

Shedding tears over

The life's long gone

While reading the obituaries

Of the Los Angeles Times

I wonder what sad sack

Writes those horror stories

Of life and death

Shaking hands

And smoking cigarettes

On the handicap ramp

To hell

The sun shows itself

Far too often

Southern California is

Patiently waiting

For the fault lines

To kiss

For the big wave

To curl like toes

She's coming

Riding a black wave

In a black dress

Waiting to break

A thunderous splash

Never heard

To be cleaned by

The polluted water

Of the pacific

Is a pipe dream to

Me and these old bastards

I've been thinking about

Why I left Oregon

Why I never stayed in

Washington

The pissing rain clouds

Of the doldrums

Have been soaking my

Mind

I'm down today

Like yesterday and

Tomorrow

Soaking the sun

On the corner of

Pine and Third

IT'S A GRIND.

It reeks like murder

the floor is blood red

And I'm thinking next week

The horses will make me more

Than the lobsters do

It's another Friday night on the

Corner of

Pine and Broadway

It's my Wednesday

I'm taking this evenings break

with a vengeance

I've been slicing away

Sloppily slicing away

At fire engine tails

In the hopes a catch myself

And bleed a bit

I was forced into this lifestyle

In and out of dead end jobs

And Micah says I can't leave

My job without another one lines up

Money changes everyone

How long does it take a

Crippled man to get on his feet

I have this urge to leave this city

To leave this life

These words

All of it

Behind

In a cloud of gun smoke

Or break smoke

I haven't seen a hummingbird

Since yesterday

And I still couldn't tell you

Who my father is

20 going on 63

The time hasn't been on my side

Since my biological clock

Went out

I wonder what it takes

To grow old

I wonder what it takes to

Die young

THE FISH HOUSE.

I've seen the allies

Of Seattle

Experienced a

Gamble of

Life and death

In hospital beds

In good ol'

Spokane

Left the pals

And heart

In Oregon

And the

Burnside Bridge

in Portland

Still owes me

Just a minute

Or two

Of my time

Took a flight

Down to Phoenix

On a steel phoenix

Towards the sun

The only thing

I fear now is

Women and guns

Welcome to

Los Angeles

California plays

A mean ambulance

And you ain't see

Poor until you

Skipped down

Skid Row

TOM AND HANK.

It's strange to remember

How exciting the city was

With a broken heart and empty wallet

After she left anyhow

It was a week maybe nine days into my move, I had

everything then

Or thought so

The job

The woman

The money

The city

The fire burning

The nightmares

more constant

Than ever

It was maybe twice or

three times that I

Actually saw her

During the week

Within the month

Deep in the ass of

The year

That has slowly become

One for the record book

I'm writing myself

Joe's hired me quickly, on College and Broadway, the

Portland State University Campus

it was November 11th

or something close to it

The manager has an olive sized mole under her nostril

And fucks the bald headed Mexican

Woman at the window

With a manakin penis

That straps to the thighs and waist

The entire kitchen

It smells like the underarms off

The fat woman who sang

On Christmas Eve on Burnside

That's a tale to tell another

Tomorrow

Joe's was downtown, a needle nesting in a haystack that

is concrete structures upon concrete structures

large enough to do the trick

when the pissing clouds drown

the doldrums

I DON'T MISS PORTLAND.

The planet crumbled

For twenty seconds

9 of which i

was terrified

Thinking the floor would

Be freed from its

Shape

And we'd be in the

Auto Shop with

Each other

Crushed, in our blood

Because our quarters

Will fail

The planet can't be saved from

Itself

Melodramatic environmentalist scum

The whiskey and wine bottles I've

Left on park benches and the beach cemetery of dreams

Never took a house out

So I guzzles my beer

The other drawn out

11 seconds

I laughed and hoped

For the worst

The buildings waving goodbye

to their shadow

welcoming the

Big wave

Standing high enough

To block out the sun

Curling like

Her hair

The last time

Our lips exchanged

Emotions

DOWN AND OUT

In the dark air

Of January the 5th

2014

We'll be cold

For minutes while

The sunless city

With open arms

Is cleaned by

The filth

We've created

Then it was ended

And the laughter was

Quickly picked up

Where it was left

The cigarettes met the lungs

the grass was rolled into

Backwoods sticks

The panic was gone

And Emilio shouted to me

"Welcome to Souther California Baby!"

Under my breath somewhere

Laced between cigarette smoke

And the smell of Tecate

"Enjoy it while it lasts"

Was said with a smile

SHAKE BABY SHAKE.

You start to feel worthless

after awhile of

feeling nothing

Momma start the car

He's found the Vicodin

like a sock

five minutes before

the Memorial Service

Wine stained trousers

and a drunk necktie

lay lifeless on the beach

Next to the shells of

habits and addictions

High tide can wait

The nap is to be had

With a vengeance

DRUNK ON THE BEACH.

It's another morning in

Southern California

An apricot sun shows

Itself on an orange tree

Illuminating plastic leaves

and the citrus spheres

It's Thursday

March 27, the year of

2014

The "What Wait" era

cats are in the allies

And I'm smoking like

A house fire

In a flat above a

Mechanics garage and some dim offices

Could it get an easier

The booze is here

The grass is growing

And going

Like smiles and strangers

I had a woman the other day

I wild woman

It's been months since I've had a woman

I made her eyes belong to me in a flurry of sweaty thrusts

and heavy breathing

The cigarettes are getting to me

I stood to attention for thirty five minutes

Before finishing in a strange place

I mashed potatoed

I did the twist

Tell me baby

Do you like it like this

Tata

And so long

IT'S NOT ALL SO BAD.

The party is primarily human beings of a Hispanic

heritage besides the Jewish man

Who's interested in how the

Coffee smells

It's not bourbon

I'm drunk in

Nathan's flat above

The auto mechanics shops

Pictures set to a fifteen second

Timer

It's my friends birthday

So I ignored my allergy to

Hops

Maybe it's a genetic thing

I should ask Julie

The laughter and loud music

Is just enough to drown

Out my screaming

Baby I'm smaller than

Grains of sand on Venice Bech

The burgundy sky

Is pulling me to bed

My beer is my beer

And my breath is my breath

Hotter than hell

And running short

FLAT BOYS.

Satisfied by simply looking at you. In a room of dead silence, calmly, quietly, waiting for the eyes, to find mine, then get lost again, in a sudoku, or art book, just knowing you are there and i am there and what we had was real, is enough.

WHEN IT'S REAL.

met up with a man

in west hollywood today

says he's a publisher

says he met Kurt Vonnegut in

Denver before he died

i wanted a cigarette the entire

conversation

but that fuck asses

down at the restaurant

claim to not have a check for me

i'm annoyed today

it's the little things

that will make a man

a madman

I just got back into

Long Beach

the sun will set soon

i'm going to watch the traffic

play rough with itself

swan dives and the 405

THE BUTCHER.

why i'm up

with the murders,

the thieves,

the drunks,

the pimps,

the whores,

the drug addicts.

we're searching

slowly

together

all dying to know

when, that next fix is coming

when dinner is served

how many licks it really takes

dancing in middle of madness,

the owl snatches up a mouse

in Cherry Avenue

i'm looking for my shoes

heading for my hat and jacket,

going to watch the 405

and think about that hummingbird

THE 4 AMER'S.

Blame yourself, for breathing

I'm throwing bones

Into bones

Empty alleys there's

a victim

Of the substance

Puddles of waterdowned blood

And whiskey

Gods been drinking

And satan brought

The powders

DON'T BLAME ME.

the liquor stores are open

all night

on every corner

until you hit Mexico

the pretty young

whore

walks alongside

the filthy old

pimp

taking backhands

and giving handjobs

making honest money

working the least

worked

loneliness is

one hell of a thing

for most it's hell

leaving one

stuck

while the hounds

yelp and wine

the hunt starts

in the reflection

of the madman

with an iron fist

white knuckles

bones thrown

fast

hard

into bones

bleed you bastard

remind yourself

you're dying

with the wolves

LA.

it was raining

again in Long Beach

i made myself

breakfast

at 1:30 PM

i do everything

too late

the hummingbird

isn't out this

morning with the

clouds and car horns

the salty air is thick

and blanketing

the sun

there is suppose

to be a flood

the rain is beating

coming down

with a vengeance

my chorizo

is cold as

a well diggers

ass

COLD CHORIZO AND HOT PLATES.

it's raining in Long Beach

which means the streets

are being cleaned from the

piss and shit and vomit

the homeless are wet

the raccoons are in hiding

i stole wine from work

so i'm drunk

i stood outside

the door for a minute

i've forgotten about work

about the drugs

the booze

alone with the rain

the muse screams

as cars pass loudly

killing puddles

while they're rebuilding

i'm fighting for the lines

one after

another

Beethoven is stabbing keys

my ears are bleeding

this is almost real

i'm grabbing my jacket

and hat

the 405 is showing a ballet

the dancers are

beautiful

and the rain is beating beats

the blood will be washed

away before morning

CITY SHOWER.

i've come to realize

i ruined my fathers life,

along with my other siblings

we devoured a man

and left a ghost

i'm sure you, like my father

had dreams once

goals,

hopes

now it's gone.

i saw it in his eyes

i was young

when he

kicked the bucket

i can notice pain though

i understood being tired

he was being beaten up

by dying dream of

lime lights

fame

money

happiness

i will never be

what i want

or

where i wanna be

enduring and running

when the muse calls

the traffic's playing

a wino's lullaby

my head is a

cinder block

and i've starting

to think

i'll never write a poem tonight

i've been drink in

DON'T HAVE A CHILD.

i see

molotov cocktails

freed to the wind

cardinals of flames

fighting gravity

for revolution

mounds of tires

burning

with the

busses

cars

buildings

bodies

trees

it's all burning

asphalt smoke

the sun

is lost

like the cause

bones and bricks

dancing

in the streets

a ballet of bruises

passionately violent

tasting blood

and liking it

disobedience is

beautiful

powerful

it's the

screaming sirens

tasting mace

dying in the street

for believing in

something

death smells like vodka

TELEVISION.

Look for the next dollar,

look for the next piece of ass,

for the next line.

silver linings

bearable truths

hah hah hah

smog sits between me and the burgundy sky

and the world won't give

anyone the time of day

don't look for anything

and

you'll find yourself

on a dock, in a port,

talking to the pigeons and seagulls

watching the boats

fighting the urge to

understand

how to properly

love the bottle

and the cunts

and the words

and the pain

and the voices

alone with the fighting crabs

and hungry birds

watch from the dock

hear the sirens scream

feel the waters

come and go

and die on that

fucking beach

ADVICE FROM A LOWLIFE.

alone in the apartment

i'm enjoying the styles of

miss Billie Holiday

drinking cheap coffee

and smoking stolen cigarettes

last night

before i made an appearance

at Gatsby's Books in Long Beach

i was overwhelmed with concern

it could've been the booming thump

of a mass hitting the bumper of a car

or the screeching tires leading up to it

or the screaming of a young woman

and her long haired boyfriend

i hurried to the window

to investigate

to kill the cat

outside the window

are two bodies shoving one another

i haven't seen a good fight in some time

they seemed to be in a flurry of emotions

while throwing themselves

around the sidewalk

i think she can take him

he looks like a whimp

before i could say "hit him"

they bolted across the road

towards the side of the street the apartment is on

i was really hoping to see violence tonight

i examined the sidewalk and the angry love birds

and noticed there aggression was subsiding

there is a body between them

a dark body slowly twitching on the sidewalk

her cries alarmed me

the broad never got hit

then the little maggot

bowed his head

it reminded me

of my fathers head

at his only brothers funeral

in Napa Idaho

i knew death was coming

i could feel her walking down the hill

i ran for my hat and jacket

then sprinted out the door and down the stairs

upon getting on the sidewalk closing the distance

between me and the unhappy lovebirds

i heard a sound i've only heard once before

the last breathes

thick black and brown fur

outlined in droplets of blood

that have splattered upon the concrete

it was a dog

a nice looking dog

besides the helplessness in held with it's eyes

drunk with concern

i thought i could save this guy

i could be a hero tonight

i extended my hand to him

signaling i wasn't going to

be harmful

then the lightning strikes

i feel a tooth in my finger

the bastard bit me

as quick as i was to save

this dying fella'

i turned on a dime

cursing him to death

i walking back towards the apartment

bleeding a stream that trumps the LA river

i spent sometime angry with the dog

DOWN AND OUT

i feel as if it were jealousy

two nights ago i laied in that street

in the hopes i'd be in his paws

he's the lucky one

there's no cars in hell

TRY AND HELP.

some nights the poems don't come out

and i laugh at my failure

i spent my day alone until

the one who's interested came along

knocking at the door

she brought a guitar and harmonica

the songs were decent

her voice sliced the air

my heart is someplace else

this living room is full of death

ANNIE I'M NOT SURE.

the pungent smell of toxic air

and cigarettes

it's like Hank said it was

but worse

herds of parasites

skwerming towards death

the aimlessly devoted humans

are so eager to love

to be loved

to feel love

is a scapegoat

hurrying into the lights

blinded

like the moths

the most expensive clubs are full

it's Valentines Day on

Hollywood Boulevard

wrinkled disgusting old men

overpowering the smell of

hot garbage and human shit

with expensive cologne and cigars

parading around tight, sexy, young

woman

that will suck them dry

as Barstow

it's all about what you have

the mindless crazies covered in

piss and shit

move about like phantoms of

the lime lights

unnoticed

unheard

unloveable

and freshly bent on stimulants

standing on the name of Billie Holliday

picking like a buzzard would a dead animal

at his neck

until skin splits and peels back

like a can of sardines

fishnetted legs and cheap high heels

hungry for a backseat and healthy buck

roaming the boulevards

the thick skinned sharks in small dresses

calling you baby

calling you into an alley

their offices

we've all come here to die

the biological clock

tics and tocs

the drunken hands reach for

the bottle

the ass

the powders

the pipes

the spinning walls

they are reaching for

the gun

as mutilated seconds pass

the third rock spins

like the finger

stirring the martini

in the hands of the

golden boy

opportunities are created

like debt and children

this world is lacking compassion

life is the punchline in a joke

never told

my solitary confinement

is a gift from the gods themselves

a holiday from the ugly creatures

the ugly voices

the ugly language

i am the rubbles of a small home

burnt to a crisp in

Eastern Washington State

piecing together charcoal dreams

in Southern California

the muse calls loudly

listen to it boy

or you'll never be great

remember

the

next

poem

is the only one

worth writing

VALENTINE'S DAY IN HOLLYWOOD.

THE SUPER BABE

My shorts fell to the floor

And I could see her cunt

Pronounced in blue panties

With a little bow on the front

She asks me

What I'm looking at

With a deep laugh

I smiled in the sunshine

As it burned like a cigarette

On my eyes

My lips split like a cigar

When I told her to

Let the cat out of the bag

She did with ease

I thought of how lucky

Those panties must be

Slipping from the buttocks

Around the gorgeous ankles

To accompany my shorts

On the squeaky patina

Naturally went on working

Together and so selfishly alone

It ended in a mess of pearls

That was cleaned with a sock

BAR FOOD

I'll be fed today somewhere

Around one or two this afternoon

What a delight it is

A greasy treat for

Another sweaty drunk

And the food is always free

And the food is always warm

Like air and pussy

THE MATTER OF FACT

It's the beginning to an end

From the sidewalk looking up at the gods

I'm drunk again

And ready to die

Baby baby

Look for me in the ash trays at you favorite bar

For those I miss

I miss dearly

The rest of you are

Trash

IM NO DADDY

She's pregnant and hates me

With crazy eyes and good legs

My mysterious scared little lady

Now the crows are singing to

Stravinsky as the skies fall

Gently to concrete gray

The rain is back

And the woman is gone

HUNGRY

Ill and fighting for breath and a roof

Pushed to my ends

The chicken broth dinners

The beef broth lunches

I'm mending a madman

Curving the pitch

And taking gulps

Call me Baby or call me asshole

Call me sunshine and kiss me goodbye

Give me a check and a bottle

Nick gave me a clock radio

That wakes up the birds

And plays Brahms

Find your guts

And follow through

www.ingramcontent.com/pod-product-compliance
Lightning Source LLC
LaVergne TN
LVHW051518070426
835507LV00023B/3170